*i*TH NK

TRANSFORMING YOUR THOUGHTS INTO GODLY BEHAVIORS

Andre Dove

ANDRE DOVE

motique media

Publishing division of Motique Momentums, LLC

www.danielaGabrielle.com/aspiring-authors

ISBN-10:0692229124
ISBN-13:9780692229125

DEDICATION

To My Dear Children,

Life has presented us with numerous challenges, some positive and some negative. My hope is that our hearts will forever be in sync despite time, distance, or feelings. You all have brought joy, motivation, and inspiration into my life in your own unique way. For that, I dedicate this book to you:

Nehemiah, D'Andre, Demetrius, and Amarys

Love,

Daddy

FOREWORD

In a time and a season where leaders are being exposed all around us, we find that even the most powerful public figures around the world are not exempt from the pressures and challenges of maintaining Godly character. John C. Maxwell defines leadership, not as position, title or tax bracket, but he defines leadership as influence.

You were called and created with influence. Each and everyone of us has a sphere of influence that we are called to wield in the earth for God. As leaders from many different walks of life, although we are meticulously prepared for the work of a leader, we are often not taught how to deal with our character along the way.

Leaders, managers, CEOs, pastors and others in the public eye are catching the media's attention for more of the wrong reasons than the right. In the age of selfies, SnapChat, Instagram, and Twitter our instant connectivity technology holds the power to make or break people on the front line. Management courses don't prepare you for dealing with the high pressured weight of bad press, negative blogs and viral videos. The good news is, the Word of God does.

Growing up in ministry, my mentor used to tell me, don't let your gift take you somewhere your character can't keep you. *i*Think by Andre Dove is a safe haven for leaders secretly battling the common issues of life. He uses his own experiences entwined with the Word of God to help bring you to a place of transformation. If you change your mind, your behaviors follow. This book is a roadmap to that change.

We all need a place where we can be vulnerable. Within the confines of these two covers is a place where you can be open before God. This is a place where God can deal with the issues that keep you from moving fully in the promises of God for your life.

Take a journey of personal transformation and let God begin a good work in you. *i*Think will challenge you to go the distance. Let your gift make room for you in the marketplace. Be prepared stand tall, because you know day by day God is positioning with poise and character to make a positive influence on the world around you.

iThink you're smart
iThink you're anointed
iThink you're strong
iThink you're enough
iThink you're equipped
iThink you're ready

iThink....it's transformation time!

Daniela Gabrielle
Best Selling Author of Fly Free: Finding the Courage to Live Without Limitations & Big Mouth Big Dreams
Orlando, Florida
www.danielaGabrielle.com

CONTENTS

1

*i*THINK

THINK LIKE CHRIST

May the mind of Christ, my Savior, Live in me from day to day, By His love and power controlling all I do and say. May the Word of God dwell richly in my heart from hour to hour, So that all may see I triumph only through His power, may the peace of God my Father rule my life in everything, that I may be calm to comfort sick and sorrowing. May the love of Jesus fill me as the waters fill the sea; Him exalting, self abasing, this is victory. May I run the race before me, Strong and brave to face the foe, looking only unto Jesus as I onward go. May His beauty rest upon me, as I seek the lost to win, and may they forget the channel, seeing only Him.

Hymn by Katie Barclay Wilkinson

This hymn expresses the transformative power of Christ in the lives of his children from day to day; it also declares the need for us to be totally dependent upon him for everything. Subsequently, as non-Christians observe us they should see that something greater is at work in our lives. Christ's purpose in coming into the world was not only to save us from our sins but also to renew our minds.

When I was attending Midwestern Baptist Theological Seminary in Kansas City, I took a pastoral counseling class. As we were discussing the behaviors that transpire between spouses in their marriage, the professor, Dr. Larry Cornine interjected by saying, "In order for behaviors to change there first must be a change in the mind." He went on to say that there's a direct correlation between how we think and the actions that follow.

As I began to reflect upon his words, I thought about my charismatic pastor who during some of his messages would always quote one of the greatest poets and lectures of the 19th century Ralph Waldo Emerson who said, "Sow a thought and you reap an action; sow an act and you reap a habit; sow a habit and you reap a character; sow a character and you reap a destiny." I lived with those words echoing in my mind for years. I've come to discover the possibility that one thought may set the course of a person's destiny.

The task of renewing our mind is first and foremost a work of the Holy Spirit in our hearts coupled with the daily consumption of God's word. Reading God's word seems to be a daunting task for us all, but it's a must if we want to see significant change in our lives. The realization that change is necessary is often met with the most resistance; however, if we desire to think differently we must yield ourselves to Christ and the power of the Holy Spirit.

The purpose of this chapter calls us to *Think like Christ*, and we will explore four questions to help us gain greater insight to the mind of Christ. These four questions are as follows:

- ♀ What did Christ think about his heavenly FATHER?

- ♀ What did Christ think about his FAMILY?

- ♀ What did Christ think about his FRIENDS?

- ♀ What did Christ think about his FOES?

These four questions are the framework of relational society. If we understand the principles that Christ employs, then our thinking will change therefore impacting society in a Godly way.

What did Christ think about his Father

As we examine the scriptures, we get a glimpse of a determined and intentional Christ with his heavenly father. When confronted by his mother and Joseph in Jerusalem as to why he didn't return home with them he says, "Did you not know I must be in my father's house?" (Luke 2:49) Here Christ examples the need for constant fellowship with the father. But it's not so with today's fathers. Fathers today are not seen to be a necessary part of the family when one looks at how they're being portrayed.

I must confess from time to time I like to watch the Maury Povich show. This show takes me through the gamut of emotions from laughing hysterically to anger and frustration at the moral decline of society. Whatever your perspective is regarding the show one thing is apparent, it reflects a definite problem in the households of America.

Contrary to popular opinion fathers are needed desperately in the lives of their children. Children are suffering and there is a great tension between the two. Listed below are ten commonly used expressions about a father. You may connect with these statements due to personal experience or you may not. And that is okay.

     ☠ I love you Daddy!

     ☠ Daddy, I want to be like you when I grow up!

     ☠ My dad is my role model.

     ☠ Dad, you're the best!

     ☠ You're not my Daddy!

     ☠ You are the father!

- ☝ I don't need you now, where have you been all my life?

- ☝ I don't know who my father is.

- ☝ When is Daddy coming home?

- ☝ I've never seen my father.

These positive and negative expressions are a reflection of a society with mixed emotions about fathers. The father has become an endangered species.

Growing up in the late 70's to early 80's, there were multiple television shows in syndication such as: *"Leave it to Beaver"*, *"The Brady Bunch"*, *"Different Strokes"*, and *"Little House on the Prairie"*, but my favorite, was *"Good Times"*. These shows portrayed fathers as providers, counselors, disciplinarians and encouragers. While watching these shows and reflecting on my own life, an overwhelming desire to have a father like those portrayed on television surfaced because my reality did not match TV's. As time passed, the qualities that were seen in these fathers seemed to be evaporating at a phenomenal rate in society. Advertisers began airing commercials that did not feature fathers further validating the emasculation of the family structure.

We see the emasculation of fathers as it is evidenced by single mothers raising their children, jails overwhelmingly filled with fathers, and churches vacant of male leadership and a male presence.

It has been said, however you view your natural father you will view God in the same manner. Another class I took in seminary was a human developmental and faith class. This class addressed the life cycle stages of development in infants. The author communicated that our conception of God comes from our parents; we see them like they are God. So then the question becomes how do we change our thinking towards God if our natural father was a negative influence in our lives? That is a challenging question that most adult children struggle to find an answer. And if you're reading this book it means you're looking for a solution to change not only how you feel about your natural father but also how you can adopt a more biblical view of God. With that being said, I believe God's word gives us the answer to this apparent difficulty.

As we look at John 17, which has been regarded as the Lord's Prayer; we find Jesus sharing some intimate time with His Father. Throughout the gospels we see Jesus participating in this common practice. What Christ is showing us is the importance of communication within a relationship. Where there is no communication there is no relationship.

When I was growing up in Chicago, I can't remember interacting with my father a lot despite the fact I had three other siblings. It just seems as if he was more absent than present. This impacted my life as it may have some of you, because as a child it is important to have that validation from your father. I can't say as we became adults our relationship changed much; fortunately, my siblings and I had a God fearing mother who believed that whatever we needed we could get from God and fellowship with other believers. The church we attended was full of men who loved God and they acted as father figures and mentors to those of us whose fathers weren't active in the lives of their children.

Whatever your relationship is with your father one thing still remains,

He is your father.

Jesus' primary focus here on earth was to complete His assigned task. His life became a road map for us to carry productive lives and healthy life-giving relationships. As He laid out a pathway to abundant life, we find His example of obedience, which as a characteristic that we should desire to take on. Obedience must be present in our lives in order to have productive relationships. Throughout your iThink journey, you will be challenged to step out of your comfort zone, restore broken relationships and heal pains of the past.

The John 17 passage speaks of a desire for fellowship to be restored. The fatherlessness of our society should pain our hearts and cause us to yearn for restoration and fellowship with our natural father as Jesus did for his heavenly Father. It seems as though our society has become accustomed to this issue of fatherlessness and that must change. For example, the television program

"*Intervention,*" captured my attention as they chronicled the lives of individuals who have experienced traumatic circumstances that caused them to become addicted to a chemical substance. This addictive substance allows them to be numb and escape the emotional pain they're experiencing.

As the origin of the substance abuse is traced, it is discovered that a divorce or some kind of sexual abuse is the culprit. When interviewed, the child often expresses the father was not present physically or he was unable to provide the emotional support needed to help them work through their issues. In many cases these cries for attention can only be heard and answered by the father. A Father's love is essential. I can say before my father died at the age of 51 we patched up our differences. We didn't have a lot of communication but he knew I loved him and he expressed that he loved me.

If your father is still alive, then explore the possibilities of rekindling your relationship. Be the first to open the lines of communication, spend time with him (i.e. fellowship) and remember life is too short too hold on to the past. Deal with the hurt, admit you're angry, let go of the resentment and forgive. Then you will be on your way to Thinking like Christ. Below is a little exercise to help you work through this process.

*i*Think Activation

List five barriers to communication with your father:

1.

2.

3.

4.

5.

List five ways to improve your communication with your father:

1.

2.

3.

4.

5.

Christ is our example not only as it relates to how one should view their father but how one views his family.

Christ's thoughts on his family

There's a common expression known to many and it goes, *"blood is thicker than water."* We hear this when someone is trying to relay the importance of family. Most would agree with the statement, but a marriage counselor introduced me to a new/old phrase *"blood is thicker than milk."* I had to pause for a moment to allow the phrase to soak in but then asked, "What does it mean?"

He explained the difference between the two statements. He stated the first implies a blood connection relationship is more important than any other relationship a person will have. While the second implies a covenant connection and whoever you are in covenant with is more important than any blood relationship you'll ever have. The differences between the two are as different as the east is from the west.

What does family mean? It means different things to different people. To some, family means division. Who should have my allegiance Mom or Dad?

In Western culture, families consist of a father, mother, and children. The Nelson's New Illustrated Bible Dictionary defines family as "a harmonious unit, where love for God and neighbor are instilled into each member." God gives instruction to the family and commands them to instill these values in their children and we should take heed to them as well.

Deuteronomy 6:6-9 New International Version states, *"And these words that I command you today shall be on your heart. You shall teach them diligently to your children, and shall talk of them when you sit in your house, and when you walk by the way, and when you lie down, and when you rise. You shall bind them as a sign on your hand, and they shall be as frontlets between your eyes. You shall write them on the doorposts of your house and on your gates."*

Over the last twenty-five years there has been a significant transition in the family structure. Single mothers and fathers occupying a dual role, the absentee parent not being involved in the child's life, and most of all the redefining of marriage between two same sex persons; consequently, all of these issues listed contribute to the demise of the family.

Jesus offers a different perspective on family in Matthew Chapter 12. He opens up with the Pharisees questioning the lawfulness of Christ and his disciple's behavior. As Jesus deals with the onslaught of questions, He's interrupted by someone who informs him that his mother and brothers are standing outside waiting to speak with him. Jesus asks the man these questions, "who is my mother? And who are my brothers?" He points to his disciples and says, "Here are my mother and my brothers. For whoever does the will of my Father in heaven is my brother and sister and mother."

The essence of what Christ thinks about family lies in obedience. If we are not obedient then we are not a part of his family. Have you heard a child say to an adult "I don't have to listen to you because you're not my mom or dad?" This viewpoint suggests that obedience implies relationship.

Jesus takes the idea of family and raises the bar. He challenges us to take inventory of our relationship with him, while asking ourselves the question, "Am I doing the will of the Father?"

To carry out his will indicates we belong to his family. And being a part of the family of God is such gif, a gift, because while he knows all our defects, disabilities, and disappointments he still decided to adopt us as his children. So it's the blood of Christ that surpasses any human relationship. So as we are reflecting on Christ and his thoughts about his father and family let's look at his thoughts on his friends.

Christ's thoughts on his Friends

In the 1980's the hip-hop group Whodini wrote a song called *"Friends"* The song's hook said "Friends, how many of us have them… Friends, ones we can depend on..." Now you might be thinking I don't have those kinds of friends or you may be saying, "I can count on one hand the amount of friends I have." Whatever your case may be it is important to know friends stick closer than a brother.

I often tell a story about moving into a new neighborhood as a kid and how my mother would tell me to get acquainted with the new neighbors, as if it was that easy. I felt somewhat awkward going to someone's house and asking "hey, do you want to come out and play?" My skepticism and lack of trust got the best of me even as a child; however, for my younger sister it was effortless. It didn't matter where we moved she could adapt quickly and by the end of the day she had plenty of friends coming to the house. She was viewed as outgoing while I gained the title of a skeptic. To this day I choose my friends carefully. Nonetheless, Christ raises the bar again and informs us in the John 15 discourse that he is the true vine and his father is the vinedresser. And he expresses the importance of producing fruit, abiding in the vine, and abiding in his love.

This type of abiding love calls for a sacrifice of one's life for his friends. Consider this; would you lay down your life for your friends? If I was asking a military member or a gang member, then the answer would be an emphatic yes. Although these two groups have differing ideologies they demonstrate a sense of unity, brotherhood, and sacrifice.

Now Jesus continues in John 15 verse 14 to elevate our understanding of friendship as he declares "you are my friends if you do what I command you" which is to say, friendship in Christ calls for obedience. Not only that, he makes the distinction between servants and friends. He says servants don't know what their master is doing but friends have the privilege of knowing what the son heard from the father.

This truth is expressed in the life of Abraham. He is affectionately known as the father of faith, the father of many nations, the father who was willing to slay his promised son, and the one whom God informed when he was getting ready to destroy the city of Sodom and Gomorrah for their wickedness. This man is called a friend of God.

The Lord said *"Shall I hide from Abraham what I am about to do, seeing that Abraham shall surely become a great and mighty nation and all the nations of the earth shall be blessed in him? For I have chosen him, that he may command his children and his household after him to keep the way of the Lord by doing righteousness and justice, so that the Lord may bring to Abraham what he has promised him. Then the Lord said, 'Because the outcry against Sodom and Gomorrah is great and their sin is very grave, I will go down to see whether they have done altogether according to the outcry that has come to me, and If not, I will know." Gen.18:17-21ESV.*

A thin line weaves itself through the first three questions of Christ's thoughts about his father, his family, and his friends. This thin line is obedience and it is fundamental for us in order to establish a relationship with Christ. Oftentimes, it seems as if we must get our horizontal relationships right before we attempt our vertical but that's not so. Christ, who is God, must be our first pursuit; once that relationship is established then we're on the road to building better horizontal relationships and transforming our thinking.

Christ's thoughts on his foes

The word "foe" is an old term used to describe an enemy. Unfortunately, at one time or another many of us have had some enemies. The question is why? Or what was the issue, which caused one's relationship to take the status of an enemy? Since the time of Cain and Abel humanity has wrestled with this dysfunctional aspect of a relationship. Bear in mind, before a person or persons were in opposition with one another they were in relationship. And most common reason for the breakdown of a relationship is an offense. To offend someone is to repeatedly disregard another's thoughts or feelings on a matter. When an individual is offended, a series of emotions begin to develop. It starts with hurt, followed by anger, after that resentment, and finally destructive behaviors toward the offender. As I stated earlier in reference to Cain and Abel, the biblical record is full of varying accounts about enemies. Not to mention, one of the most noted adversaries, the devil.

Since his forced exodus out of heaven, he's main agenda is to thwart the plan of God by using the very ones God came to save which are you and I. I know as I look at my life. I often wonder, "Is the devil winning the battle?' **The answer is No!**

The Devil's plan is to keep us fighting against one another and he thinks that it's full proof. But Jesus addresses how we should respond to our enemies. As stated earlier, enemies become enemies because an individual was hurt, angered, and resentful. We must consider; how God is calling us to respond to our enemies. Furthermore we must examine how he responded to his?

There are two biblical examples that demonstrate how God intends for us to respond to our enemies. First, let's examine his message on the Sermon on the Mount found in Matthew 5:43-48 and then we will focus on his crucifixion at Calvary.

The Sermon on the Mount is one of Jesus' most impactful and heart wrenching sermons that challenge us to transform our thinking.

"You have heard that it was said, you shall love your neighbor and hate your enemy. But I say to you, Love your enemies and pray for those who persecute you, so that you may be sons of your Father who is in heaven. For he makes his sun rise on the evil and on the good and sends rain on the just and on the unjust. For if you love those who love you, what reward do you have? Do not even the tax collectors do the same? And if you greet only your brothers, what more are you doing than others? Do not even the Gentiles do the same? You therefore must be perfect, as your heavenly Father is perfect." Matthew 5:43-48 English Standard Version
As it relates to this passage, one commentator mentioned that, "One manifestation of love for enemies

will be in prayer; praying for an enemy and loving him will prove mutually reinforcing. The more love, the more prayer; the more prayer, the more love." My prayer for others and myself is to follow the example of scripture and realize that love for our enemies is manifested by our prayers for them.

Jesus illustrates this point masterfully as he was being crucified. When it seemed as if he lost and his enemies had won, while enduring the intensity of the stakes being driven through his hands and feet, the crown of thorns pressed into his head while being beaten severely, he says "Father, forgive them for they know not what they do." This was not just a one-time prayer. As they continued to inflict pain on the Savior, he kept praying "Father, forgive them for they know not what they do." He was enduring this unjust torture for you and me. We deserved this cruel punishment yet he took our place and all he asks of us is to forgive our enemies.

Are you willing to follow the example of Jesus and pray father, forgive them for they know not what they are doing. Despite the pain and agony you've endured, Christ's answer is Pray! Pray! Pray!

As we challenge ourselves to *"Think Like Christ"* we must remember that total reliance on the father is necessary for a great relationship, blood is thicker than milk, obeying God is a must to be his friend, and showing love for your enemies through prayer will prove you love God. Be encouraged by the Apostle Paul in *Philippians 4:13 "I can do all things through him who strengthens me."*

*i*Think Activation

Take the time to list five of your enemies and commit to praying for them until God changes your heart towards them.

_____

_____

_____

_____

_____

Prayer: *Lord, I commit myself to love my enemies through prayer. Help me to have a heart of forgiveness as you strengthen me. In you all things are possible. In Jesus name I pray Amen.*

2

*i*TH💡NK

THINK GRACE

---

*The story is told of John Newton the famous
abolitionist, clergyman, and hymn writer who wrote the
hymn "Amazing Grace." A few years before Mr.
Newton died; a friend was having breakfast with him.
Their custom was to read from the bible after the meal.
Because Newton's eyes were growing dim, his friend
would read, and then Newton would comment briefly on
the passage. That day the selection was from 1
Corinthians 15. When the words "by the grace of God I
am what I am" were read, Newton was silent for
several minutes. Then he said, "I am not what I ought
to be. How imperfect and deficient I am! I am not what
I wish to be, although I abhor that which is evil and
would cleave to what is good. I am not what I hope to
be, but soon I shall put off mortality, and with it all sin.*

Though I am not what I ought to be, nor what I wish to be, nor yet what I hope to be, I can truly say I am not what I once was: a slave to sin and Satan. I can heartily join with the apostle and acknowledge that by the grace of God I am what I am!"

What an amazing eulogy that John Newton presents of himself. How often do we take time to inventory our lives? Most often this assessment takes place at the end of life, as we are breathing our last breath. While this is acceptable and a normal process in death, why wait till then? For example, if you hold a position where inventory is a must or you're in charge of replacing or stocking supplies, you understand its importance. If things are not at your disposal a delay is certain. This poses a problem for you, the distributer, and also the customer; and so it is with God. He is calling us to a higher place, not just to do inventory, but also to investigate our lives.

This personal investigation into our life is tough and necessary; howbeit, God does not require us to do this alone, but enlists the assistance of the Holy Spirit.

As we begin to talk about grace, it's apparent that we need a daily injection of it in our lives. *Think Grace* is a command for us to remember the need to apply it in every situation we encounter.

What is Grace?
In the Greek language, the word for grace is *"charis."* This word is commonly defined by many as the unmerited favor of God; while this is true, the more

exhaustive definition is as follows: *"of the merciful kindness by which God, exerting his holy influence on souls, turns them to Christ, keeps, strengthens, increases them in Christian faith, knowledge, affection, and kindles them to the exercise of the Christian virtues."*

What an exhilarating expression of God's grace, which states, out of his merciful kindness he endows undeserving persons like you and me. He accomplishes a powerful work with regard to this grace given to us and here they are:

1. He exerts his holy influence on souls.
2. He turns them to Christ.
3. He keeps them.
4. He strengthens them.
5. He increases them in Christian faith.
6. He increases them in knowledge.
7. He increases them in affection.
8. He kindles them to the exercise of the Christian virtues.

God and God alone initiate the work of grace. His sovereign decree is to give grace to whomever he will. According to Ephesians 2:10 which says, "For we are his workmanship created in Christ Jesus for good works, which God prepared beforehand, that we should walk in them."

The Apostle Paul is a great example of God's grace being applied to someone's life. His commendations include writing two-thirds of the New Testament, planting many churches, mentoring and instructing countless persons, being arrested multiple times for preaching the Gospel, and often receiving many afflictions from various opponents of his.

But Paul was not always an advocate for Christ and his message; as a matter of fact, he vehemently protested against anyone who believed or proclaimed the message of Christ. In the book of Acts chapter 8 and 9, Paul who is formally known as Saul is seen giving his approval of the execution of Stephen. He was known to invade homes dragging men and women off committing them to prison, and breathing threats and murder against the disciples of the Lord.

In Acts 9, we see the beginning of Saul's transformation. He asks the high priest for letters to the synagogues in Damascus so if he found any people belonging *"to the Way,"* (that's what they were called before being called Christians at Antioch) he might bring them back to Jerusalem bound. But on his way to Damascus to execute his plan, Christ initiated and implemented His plan for Saul's life.

Can you imagine being taken into custody, interrogated and struck with blindness by Jesus Christ? This is Grace in action. It seems extreme but some people need extreme occurrences to take place in their life in order for God to get their attention. When God chooses you, you cannot resist him. You may try; however, he will make your life so uncomfortable that you'll see it his way and submit to his will. If you need another example, read the story of Jonah of the runaway Prophet whom God teaches a lesson about grace.

After Saul's conversion and name change along with many trials and imprisonments we get a better understanding of what Paul meant when he stated in 1Corinthians 15:10 "But by the grace of God I am what I am, and his grace toward me was not in vain." Understand this to whomever God applies his grace there is always a purpose and plan.

Grace opened the way for Saul to hear the Gospel. God not only has grace for us, but he says we need to have grace for one another. So how do we put into action this grace to one another?

Grace for one another.

Since God alone initiates grace, how do we as people of God express it in our human relationships? We have the tendency as people to give and withhold based on merit, but if Christ lives in us it is our duty to imitate him in all we do. If we examine our lives, we have to admit that we have received grace from others knowing we didn't deserve it.

Let's consider marriage for a moment, it's the most intimate of all human relationships and oftentimes the most challenging. It is understood by many that the majority of problems in a relationship stem from the lack of communication and unresolved issues. Why is it difficult for couples to extend grace to one another? Could it be the familiarity with each other? What about pride? Or is it just that they don't want to? Whatever the reason, if we can't offer it in the most intimate human relationship then those on the outside don't have a chance. Grace doesn't see color, male or female, rich or poor, neither young nor old. It is just grace.

Paul also says, the gospel is the key component to grace being applied to one's life. If you're married look at your spouse, we need to see them and their imperfections through the lenses of Christ's substitutionary death. Just as he died, was buried, and raised for you so it is with your spouse.

In summation, in order for us to fulfill the command to *Think Grace,* we must be totally dependent upon it in our own lives then we are able to give it to others. Looking in the mirror at our own sinfulness will allow us to say as Paul said...I am what I am only by the Grace of God.

*i*Think Activation

As we embrace God's grace in our lives, we must be an extension of His grace on earth. How can you extend grace to those around you on a consistent basis?

Spouse/Significant Other _____

_____

Family _____

_____

Co-workers/Colleagues _____

_____

Neighbors _____

_____

Friends _____

_____

Random Strangers _____

_____

Prayer: Lord, thank you for your Grace that's been extended to such a person as myself, please help me to demonstrate to others what you have demonstrated to me all the days of my life. And when I encounter someone undeserving please let me remember to *Think Grace!*

3

*i*TH**I**NK

TAKE IT OFF

I want a principle within of watchful, godly fear,
A sensibility of sin, a pain to feel it near.
I want the first approach to feel of pride or wrong
desire,
To catch the wandering of my will, and quench the
kindling fire.

From Thee that I no more may stray, no more Thy
goodness grieve,
Grant me the filial awe, I pray, the tender conscience
give.
Quick as the apple of an eye, O God, my conscience
make;
Awake my soul when sin is nigh, and keep it still awake.

Almighty God of truth and love, to me Thy power impart;
The mountain from my soul remove, the hardness from my heart.
O may the least omission pain my reawakened soul,
And drive me to that blood again, which makes the wounded whole.

Charles Wesley (Hymns and Sacred Poems 1749)

What a tremendous hymn written by the great hymn writer and clergyman Charles Wesley. It is stated that he composed six thousand hymns and one of them being, the popular **"Hark, the Herald Angels Sing."** This song has been sung and heard around the world for hundreds of years. Take a moment to meditate and reflect on these words that proclaim the gospel of Jesus Christ.

Hark! the herald angels sing

Glory to the new-born King!

Peace on earth and mercy mild,

God and sinners reconciled.

Joyful all ye nations rise,

Join the triumph of the skies,

With the angelic host proclaim

Christ is born in Bethlehem!

Hail the heaven-born Prince of Peace!

Hail the Sun of Righteousness!

Light and life to all he brings,

Risen with healing in his wings.

Mild, he lays his glory by;

Born, that man no more may die,

Born to raise the sons of earth,

Born to give them second birth.

Not only does this well known hymn express the gospel, but also the aforementioned hymn expresses our continual need of this gospel message. You can hear the hymn writer's heart cry for God not to let any sin disrupt their fellowship and so it is for us to we long for that kind of relationship.

How do we ascertain a fellowship with such a sovereign God? Is it possible for the infinite to interact with the finite? Does the one who exemplifies the personification of purity want to dwell with the impure? And finally, how does the depraved commune with the Holy One?

  Consider this, a great number of us are familiar with the congestion, frustration, and anticipation of being in an airport with its frequent occurrences of flight delays and cancellations. In addition, we are accustomed to the weight requirements on luggage and the quantity that we can transport. Nothing is more time consuming and grueling than having to go through airport security. There are long lines, impatient people, and fussy babies who have no idea what's going on.

Along with that, if you're running late, you also experience the overwhelming anxiety of potentially missing your flight. And if you've ever missed a flight you know what I'm talking about.

Airport security has obviously increased since the terrorist attacks on 9/11. In 2001 the government established the TSA (Transportation Security Administration) to ensure the safety of those traveling. With that being said, in order to board the plane you must pass through the security checkpoint. At this area, you are required to present your identification with your boarding pass. Then you are instructed to put your carryon baggage on the x-ray scanner and remove certain accessories such as shoes, watches, wallets, keys etc. so that those items can be scanned. You are further instructed to notify the TSA agent of any metal that you might have internally due to any reconstructive surgery before you pass through the scanner. The purpose of this request is to make certain that you are not a threat to those that are traveling on the same flight.

In Ephesians 4:20-32, Paul deals with the idea of communing with the Holy One and he brings awareness to the church at Ephesus the need to remove certain behaviors in order that the communion with God is not disrupted.

In our airport illustration, it suggests the importance of removing necessary items to ensure that we don't pose a threat to those traveling while also allowing you to put those items back on after passing through the scanner. Paul in Ephesians 4:20, implies the equivalent with certain stipulations. He instructs the Ephesians to remove some things without putting them on again, because they represent your former manner of life and is corrupt through deceitful desires. Although the TSA agent says you're not a threat to the passengers, Paul communicates that you are a threat to those around you because you misrepresent your new life in Christ. In addition to that, he declares there must be an acknowledgeable difference in the way you walk; see verses 17-18: *"Now this I say and testify in the Lord, that you must no longer walk as the Gentiles do, in the futility of their minds. They are darkened in their understanding, alienated from the life of God because of the ignorance that is in them due to their hardness of heart."*

The term Gentiles was used in the 1st century to identify persons as foreigners or it applied to any other culture group that was not Jewish. Paul then points out the Gentiles' walk & life as being darkened. Their morals did not line up with Christ, which caused them to be alienated from a life with God. And that is due to their pride. Ponder these questions for a moment.

Is your life darkened, even though you wake up daily to see the sun shining, do you still feel like there's not enough light? Are you fascinated with the quantity of friends that you have but still feel like someone is missing? When an inward desire prompts you to go to church, do you resist it and say "I'll go next Sunday? Do you find yourself taking more pleasure in things that gratify the flesh with no concern about God? Or maybe you claim to be a follower of Christ but are ensnared by the trappings of the enemy and need to be rescued?

Don't get me wrong, sin is fun, enjoyable, exciting, and thrilling etc. But it only last for a moment and brings with it serious consequences. Paul the apostle gives us some help for our situation. He says the first thing we must do is to be willing to leave our old life behind (see verse 22).

Before I joined the United States Air Force, I thought my life was pretty good. I had my own apartment and car. I also shared the apartment with a couple of roommates. One day everything turned upside down. One of my roommates fell asleep while boiling hot dogs and almost burned down the apartment and of course we got kicked out. We moved out to another buddy's house, which only lasted a week or two until he notified us he was being evicted. Finally, I said, we can stay at my mom's house. We really didn't want to stay in the house we wanted to pitch a tent and stay in the back yard. So we took my friends' brother's tent and put it up in my mom's backyard.

We thought we had it made until his brother came a couple hours later demanding his tent back because we didn't ask. He sat us down. And said how long can you guys do this? You need to do something different with your lives. There is not a woman out there that would want a couple of losers like you. Then he said, "Ya'll need to go to the military. The pay is good and the food is great." That's all we needed to hear. We went down to the recruiter's office; signed up with the

Air Force and a couple of weeks later we were off into the wild blue yonder.

During our basic training, the MTI's (Military Training Instructors) informed us when we returned home we would see our old friends doing the same ole things without having made any progression and they were right. Upon returning from basic training, we saw exactly what the instructor said then we realized the importance of leaving the old self behind.

The second task in "Taking it off" requires the mind to be renewed. Paul in the book of Romans 12:2 says *"Do not be conformed to this world, but be transformed by the renewal of your mind, that by testing you may discern what is the will of God, what is good and acceptable and perfect."* The only way we will know what is good and perfect is that we have a God consciousness. Things that we see, read, and hear influence the way we think. Someone told me a long time ago; "If you put garbage into your mind then you will get garbage in return." Consequently, we must ask ourselves. What are we putting into our minds? Are we reminiscing about our old life and the temporary excitement it brought to us?

Finally Paul commands us in v. 24 to put on our new life, which was created after the likeness of God in true righteousness and holiness. After I graduated basic training, I realized I was a different man, with a different mindset, and a different life. Upon I reported to my new duty station, I was extremely excited because I never imagined my life would be so different.

For those of you who are in the military or have family members who serve our country, you can share in the enthusiasm of seeing that member go through the metamorphosis of what they used to be and now who they have become. Parents, maybe you experience this in the child you sent off to college, as time passed you noticed the transformation in him/her especially when they walked across the stage to receive their degree. In the same way, that emotion and celebratory response takes place in heaven when someone comes to faith in our Lord Jesus Christ.

In Luke 15:1-32, which I call "The Trilogy of the Lost" every time something or someone has been found the natural response is to have a celebration. Then, it would suffice to say; that earth does what heaven has done when we put on our new life.

But it doesn't stop with the celebration, Paul gives us nine responsibilities in vs. 25-32 that we should adhere to in order to stay in proper fellowship with God:

- Stop lying and tell the truth to everyone
- Be angry and do not sin. Don't give room to the devil
- Stop stealing and work honestly with your own hands. So that you can give to those in need.
- Stop using foul and or abusive language. Let your words be an encouragement to one another.
- Don't bring sorrow to the Holy Spirit because he is the one that has identified you as his own.
- Get rid of all bitterness, wrath, anger, clamor, slander along with malice.

- ☼ Be Kind
- ☼ Be tenderhearted
- ☼ Forgive one another as God in Christ forgave you!

These last nine imperatives could never be done without the help of the Holy Spirit. So as we see the transformation occurring in our lives, it should intensify our focus all the more toward God.

*i*Think Activation

As we open our lives to transformation, we must be willing to come face-to-face with the areas we struggle in and submit them to God. Write about the areas you are struggling in and commit those vulnerabilities to the Lord.

_____
_____
_____
_____

Prayer: Lord, we acknowledge your presence, your grace and mercy. We admit our inability to accomplish this great task without the Holy Spirit. We confess our sins and accept your forgiveness; as we forgive those who have wronged us. Thank you for your blessings and your strength. Help us to remember to *"Take it off!"* We pray this prayer in the Strong name of Jesus. Amen.

4

i THINK

SET YOUR MIND

Because your mind is where the problem is, in the first place!

Dr. Rosen "A Beautiful Mind"

One of my favorite movies of all time is the movie entitled *"A Beautiful Mind."* It is based on the true story of the Nobel Laureate recipient John Forbes Nash Jr. This honor was bestowed upon him for his work in the field of economics in 1994. The movie portrays John Nash as a genius mathematician struggling with a mental disorder called paranoid schizophrenia. Let me add before we move on, this chapter will not deal with schizophrenia, its causes, effects, or symptoms etc. I just love the movie.

In her Biography of John Nash with the same name as the movie, Sylvia Nasar describes Mr. Nash not only as an extremely gifted mathematician but she also characterizes him as an arrogant, socially inept, rude, and abrasive individual. It is stated that he has changed some of those negative stereotypes attributed to him. Like Sylvia, I'm sure many of us have encountered persons of that type on a daily basis. Nevertheless, the question becomes, what is the fundamental issue?

Since this book is about transforming our thoughts into Godly behaviors and the focus of this chapter is about setting your mind then the issue is profoundly stated in the opening quote by Dr. Rosen, because your mind is where the problem is in the first place. Wow, what a statement. It can be said that the majority of people's issues can be traced back to their belief about themselves.

Paul deals with the reality of the intense struggle of the mind and the flesh of the believer. He says in the most familiar passage of scripture found in Romans chapter seven. I'll paraphrase it, "I don't do what I should do but I do what I don't want to do." The apparent struggle with sin causes all of us to realize the problem is bigger than we can handle. I also realized as I was reading chapters 1-11, a person's behavior gives an observer insight into their thought life. That is to say, what you see me doing tells you what I've been thinking.

Romans 12: 1-3 gives us added instruction that will provide clarity on the problem and how we should handle it. In order to *"Set your mind"* there are three major movements that will aid you in achieving the purpose toward Godly thinking:

1. We must have a proper view of self.
2. We must exhibit sound judgment.
3. We must utilize the faith given to us.

We must have a proper view of self.

Physical

In a society that judges people based on their physical appearance, a countless number of women starve themselves. Hollywood has seemingly defined what true beauty represents. At the same time, others see plastic surgery as a viable option and some use prescription medications to help them obtain their ideal look. While it is important to maintain good health and eating habits, we can't continue to allow society to misrepresent and judge what is ideal. It is more important to possess a biblical worldview than to fall into the trap of a fragmented secular humanistic worldview.

Psalms 139:14-16 proclaims, "I praise you, for I am fearfully and wonderfully made. Wonderful are your works; my soul knows it very well. My frame was not hidden from you, when I was being made in secret, intricately woven in the depths of the earth. Your eyes saw my unformed substance; in your book were written, every one of them, the days that were formed for me, when as yet there was none of them."

How awesome are the words of David in this Psalm? God used this marred, tainted warrior to pen such awe inspiring words that would allow us to see God's majestic power in creating each one of us. Moreover, God says himself that everything he created was very good. So not only are we enamored by the physical but often times captivated by the spiritual.

*i*Think Activation

It's time to transform any negative thoughts that you have about your physical image. Replace those thoughts with what the Word of God has to say about you.

What You Think	What God Thinks

Spiritual

It doesn't matter how long you've been in church or around it. At some time or another, you've encountered those persons who are deemed to be super spiritual. You can recognize them afar off. They are the first to arrive at church, they don't have a sense of humor, they are critical of the less fortunate, and they have supposedly walked with the Lord for a long time. And my all time favorite, they live a life free of sin. I like to call those individuals the spiritual elite.

This mentality is more prevalent among clergy today. They're surrounded by the security detail at the church and it takes an act of congress to talk with them. I wonder do they take the security detail with them to the grocery store or the movies. I think not. These celebrity preachers have bought into their own hype and have contaminated a new generation of preachers who seek fame and fortune while disregarding what Jesus said in Matthew 20:26-28 "But whoever would be great among you must be your servant, and whoever would be first among you must be your slave, even as the son of Man came not to be served but to serve, and to give his life as a ransom for many"

John's gospel records Jesus giving his disciples an example of the message that he has been declaring for some time (see John 13:2-4) "During supper, when the devil had already put it into the heart of Judas Iscariot, Simon's son, to betray him, Jesus, knowing that the Father had given all things into his hands, and that he had come from God and was going back to God, rose from supper. He laid aside his outer garments, and taking a towel, tied it around his waist. Then he poured water into a basin and began to wash the disciples' feet and to wipe them with the towel that was wrapped around him."

What a marvelous expression of servitude given by the greatest preacher, pastor, bishop, evangelist, and prophet who ever lived. This is the King of Kings bending down and washing his disciples' feet. Let that marinate for a moment. Know ask yourselves, why are we not seeing that type of sacrifice among clergy today?

As I'm writing this chapter, I'm reading the book called "Greater" by Stephen Furtick Senior Pastor of Elevation Church. He states in chapter nine regarding this passage of scripture "Only insecure people need to assert their power. Jesus knew who he was; he knew where he had come from and knew where he was going." So serving was not in issue for him. Consequently, if we don't have a proper view of self we will fall into the trap that has fooled so many in times past.

Christ calls us to model his behavior. Clergymen! Get rid of your security detail and pick up a towel.

The cause of this celebrity focus lies within your heart. The Apostle Paul challenges us (see Romans 12:3) not think more highly of ourselves than we ought to think but we are to think with sober judgment. This leads me to our second major movement on our way to setting our mind towards Godly thinking.

We must exhibit sound judgment.

Imagine being remembered as a valiant warrior who won many great battles? How about being a twelve year old kid fighting a bear and lion to protect your father's sheep or fighting a nine-foot tall giant named Goliath? Well that was King David. Anointed at a young age by a prophet sent by God, David was known as a man after God's own heart.

Fast forward some years and here we are at the precipice of transition from life to death. But before David takes his last breath, he leaves Solomon with some instructions as he prepares to assume the throne. He says... "Be strong, and show yourself a man, and keep the charge of the Lord your God, walking in his ways and keeping his statutes, his commandments, his rules, and his testimonies, as it is written in the Law of Moses, that you may prosper in all that you do and wherever you turn, that the Lord may establish his word that he spoke concerning me, saying, 'If your sons pay close attention to their way, to walk before me in faithfulness with all their heart and with all their soul, you shall not lack a man on the throne of Israel.' (See 1 Kings 2:2-4)

After such an intimate dialogue between a father and his son, David dies. The Kingdom is now in the hands of Solomon. How would you handle such responsibility? It is agreed by many biblical scholars that Solomon was between the ages of 16-20 when he began to reign. Most of us can remember saying as young teenagers. I can't wait till I get out of the house. I won't run my house like my parents did. Or maybe you're an associate minister who says I can't wait till I get my own church things will be different.

It's always easier to say what you would do when you're observing than it is when you're on the job. I'm sure Solomon watched his father rule for years and witnessed he father's dependence on God. To rule this massive kingdom effectively Solomon knew he needed sound judgment and God knew it as well. At Gibeon, where Solomon went to worship, the Lord speaks to him in a dream and asks; what shall I give you? (see 1Kings 3: 5) Wow! I can only imagine the things we would ask for if God presented us with that question. And like many of us, I'm sure Solomon pondered the question for a moment before responding. Nevertheless, he has a reality check about his age as well as, the weighty responsibility of governing a kingdom. He says, "Give your servant therefore an understanding mind to govern your people, that I may discern between good and evil, for who is able to govern this great people?" God is pleased with Solomon's humble heart in that he didn't ask selfishly neither did he ask for retribution on his enemies. Therefore, he gave Solomon all he didn't ask for and make him the wisest man that ever lived.

Humility is what God wants, not just in the beginning of our lives but throughout. Having a humble heart will always allow us to make the sound decisions.

We must utilize the faith given to us.

The third major movement in setting your mind is faith. It is essential for us to realize that faith is a gift from God. Not only that, the utilization of our faith requires us to offer ourselves as a living sacrifice. The Apostle Paul states in Rom. 12:1 "I appeal to you therefore, brothers, by the mercies of God to present your bodies as a living sacrifice, holy and acceptable to God, which is your spiritual worship."

Presenting ourselves as a living sacrifice requires faith. Who knows better than anyone about offering a living sacrifice than Abraham the father of faith? In Genesis 18 Abraham is visited by three men who inform him that this time next year Sarah his wife will finally have the child the Lord had promised twenty four years earlier. As time passes Sarah gives birth to the promised child and they name him Isaac, which means laughter.

Even though it took many years for the promise to be realized, Abraham and Sarah finally are able to hold the bundle of joy in their arms. Has God promised you something that you're still waiting for it to manifest? If so, continue to wait and believe. The Lord keeps his promises. Numbers 23:19 affirms a characteristic about God. It says, "God is not man, that he should change his mind. Has he said, and will he not do it? Or has he spoken, and will he not fulfill it?" If you truly believe the Lord has spoken a promise in your life then you must hold on to it with everything you have. It will come to pass. It does not matter what it looks like. It does not matter what other people say. Hold on to the word of God. That's what Abraham and Sarah did. Even with a couple of bumps along the way, God fulfilled his word.

After Abraham receives his promised son, suddenly, God does the unthinkable. He commands Abraham to take his son that he waited so long for, the son he loved so deeply and offer him up as a burnt offering. I'm sure Abraham was saying, "Are you kidding me, I waited twenty plus years for this child now you want me to burn him up?" It didn't matter to Abraham what God was asking of him, he believed God had it all under control.

In obedience to God, Abraham proceeded up the mountain, tied his son to the altar and took out his knife to slay him. Right at that crucial moment, the angel of Lord called him from heaven and told him, "Do not lay your hand on the boy or do anything to him, for now I know that you fear God, seeing you have not withheld your son, your only son, from me. And Abraham lifted up his eyes and looked, and behold, behind him was a ram, caught in a thicket by his horns. And Abraham went and took the ram and offered it up as a burnt offering instead of his son." (See Genesis 22)

What a faith journey! Do we love our lives that much that we're unwilling to offer ourselves as a living sacrifice to God? Can we like Abraham willingly offer that which we love so much and give it to him? God wants all of you and me. And God has given us the tool to make it happen, faith!

*i*Think Activation

Think about a time that God challenged you to make a major sacrifice, like Abraham. How did it work out? How has that impacted the way you think about faith?

_____

_____

_____

_____

_____

_____

_____

_____

_____

_____

_____

_____

Prayer: Lord, I need your help on this journey of setting my mind. Help me to have a proper view of self. Let me see myself as you see me. Give me wisdom not to walk in pride and the faith to believe that you have it all under control. Help me to realize that no matter what it looks like and no matter what people say, your word will come to pass. Thank you for your grace and mercy in Jesus name. Amen.

5

*i*TH🔅NK

SERVE THE LORD

A blessing for you—will you take it?
Choose ye today;
A word from the heart—will you speak it?
Choose ye today:
Will you believe, or your Savior neglect?
Will you receive, or His mercy reject?
Pause, ere you answer, oh, pause and reflect—
Choose ye today.

Hymn by Fanny Crosby

Four years ago America embarked upon a historic moment by electing the first black President of the United States. The slogan of the President's campaign was *"Change we can believe in"* with the chant *"Yes we can."* Despite your political views about the election in 2008 and where you believe we are four years later, it is more important to realize the impact your vote will have on future generations. Having the ability to vote and or choose a President is a fundamental right of every American. With that being said, there is a more dominant issue at hand and it's an eternal one. Every believer must understand there is one who's greater than President Obama and Governor Mitt Romney. His name is Jesus Christ our Lord! While you may be saying "duh" I know that; the question is how does that revelation manifest itself in your daily walk?

The above hymn gives us insight to a reality of an eternal destination that is contingent upon what we believe about our Lord and what he has revealed to us about ourselves. This requires us to make a decision. One verse that comes to mind that may be familiar to all. The main character is Joshua. He has taken the helm in leading the children of Israel to the promise land after the death of Moses. He says in Joshua 24:15 "Choose this day whom you will serve...But as for me and my house, we will serve the Lord."
Oftentimes, we don't hear about the intense struggles that Joshua encountered as he was leading Israel on this journey to the promise land. But as I was reading the book from beginning to end six principles emerged that I believe will help us fulfill the command to "Serve the Lord."

- ☀ Re-acquaint us with the God of the Bible
- ☀ Recognize the severity of sin
- ☀ Recite God's goodness to your children
- ☀ Remember God has an inheritance for you
- ☀ Renew your commitment to following God
- ☀ Realize the Bible will be a witness against you

Re-acquaint us with the God of the Bible

Who is this God of the Bible? Does he conflict with the image we have of him? Does he differ with what we've heard preached throughout the years? I believe the answer is yes. Why? Because what we currently hear on television and in some churches today is a view that is contradictory to what the Bible says. In order to truly know someone, you must spend time communicating with them. So what does God say about himself? It is impossible to list everything but here are a few things he says about himself.

1. I am God Almighty **Genesis 17:1**
2. I am who I am **Exodus 3:14**
3. I am the Lord God who brought you out of Egypt, out of the house of slavery
   Exodus 20:1-2
4. Thus says the Lord, the King of Israel and his Redeemer, the Lord of hosts: "I am the first and I am the last; besides me there is no god.
   Isaiah 44:6
5. Remember the former things of old; for I am God, and there is none like me...
   Isaiah 46:9

6. See now that I, even I, am he, and there is no god beside me; I kill and I make alive; I wound and I heal; and there is none that can deliver out of my hand.

Deut. 32:39

7. But let him who boasts boast in this, that he understands and knows me, that I am the Lord who practices steadfast love, justice, and righteousness in the earth, for in these things I delight, declares the Lord.

Jeremiah 9:24

8. Behold, I am the Lord, the God of all flesh. Is there anything too hard for me?

Jeremiah 32:27

9. For I am the Lord; I will speak the word that I will speak, and it will be performed. It will no longer be delayed, but in your days, O rebellious house, I will speak the word and perform it, declares the Lord.

Ezekiel 12:25

10. And my holy name I will make known in the midst of my people Israel, and I will not let my holy name be profaned anymore. And the nations shall know that I am the Lord, the Holy One in Israel.

Ezekiel 39:7

Now that you have heard God speak for himself about himself, the question becomes does it harmonize with what you thought you knew about him? If it does great then keep moving forward but if it not; I urge you to spend more time reading the Bible to get to know him better. Joshua and the children of Israel knew God in an intimate way but that's not all. They understood that God hated disobedience. Which leads us to the next principle; we must recognize the severity of sin.

Recognize the severity of sin

In this post-modern era, where morality is on a rapid decline, truth is relative and sin in some circles of the evangelical world is no longer being preached; there must be a resurgence of biblical literacy. I heard someone say not too long ago, "Oh! It's a forgivable sin" What!

How far has Christianity fallen when believers can so haphazardly declare with no fear, the above statement? Is it because we've lost respect for God? Or do we not fear that God will deal with us because of Grace? Ask Achan (read Joshua 6 & 7). Here's a man who just seen the wonder of God on display as the walls of Jericho fell and the people were defeated. God gives specific instruction to Joshua and the children of Israel not to take of those things that are devoted for destruction. But when Achan sees the beautiful cloak, the silver and gold, he greatly desires them and took them to his tent and hid them underneath. As the time came for the children of Israel to enter into battle with Ai they were defeated. Joshua fell on his face and inquired of the Lord. And God said, "Israel has sinned" He then tells Joshua to bring the clans, households, and finally the men. Whoever is found with the devoted things (see Joshua 7:14-15) "shall be burned with fire, he and all that he has because he has transgressed the covenant of the Lord"

So as Joshua has the tribes passed man by man Achan appears before him and Joshua ask in verse 19 "My son, give glory to the Lord God of Israel and give praise to him. And tell me now what you have done; don't hide it from me." Achan tells Joshua what he did. Joshua sends messengers to see if the story checks out. The messengers find the devoted things exactly where Achan said they would be then they take Achan along with the cloak, the silver and gold, his sons and daughters, oxen and donkeys, and all he had to the Valley of Achor. Joshua says, "Why did you bring trouble on us? Today trouble will be brought on you." And so they stoned and burned everything and everybody in the presence of all Israel.

Achan's sin just like ours does not only affect the individual but it affects everyone associated with them. It's like the pebble that is thrown into the water the ripple effects spread out wide. God is the same yesterday today and forever more. We don't know how God will deal with our sin and us but be assured that he will deal with us. God dealt with Achan in front of all of Israel so that they would know God means what he says. I'm sure the people of Israel talked about the judgment of God on Achan and his family for a while.

1 John 3:4-6, 8 says, "Everyone who makes a practice of sinning also practices lawlessness; sin is lawlessness. You know that he appeared to take away sins, and in him there is no sin. No one who abides in him keeps on

sinning; no one who keeps on sinning has either seen him or known him. Whoever makes a practice of sinning is of the devil, for the devil has been sinning from the beginning." Sin is serious to God and should be serious to those who say they are followers of Christ. James the brother of Jesus proclaims in the epistle that bears his name that if you keep the whole law and offend in one point you're guilty of the whole.

Let me remind you, just because Grace has been initiated does not mean that God will not allow us to experience the consequences of our actions. Meditate on that for a moment.

Recite God's goodness to your children

We all know the saying that "bad news travels fast" If you watch the news at all you know how true that statement is. It seems they only report bad news. How often do you hear about something good? We have the best news in the world. Why aren't we sharing it?

Parents how often do you tell your children of the good news of Jesus Christ or what he has accomplished in your life? Sure, we'll talk about God throughout the day and sometimes we'll witness to an unknown individual. But why is it so hard to communicate to our children God's blessings? More importantly, why does scripture emphasize the need to relay God's word to our children? Here are few reasons why God commands parents to express the word of God to their children. It builds a foundation of the knowledge of God in their heart, while also showing the children that their total dependence must be on God, and it helps them to value and know they are carriers of the gospel to future generations.

Conveying this message to our children is not solely verbal but it incorporates a commitment of our lifestyle. Unfortunately, I can't say that both of my parents were committed to this task; however, I am grateful for my mother's sacrifice as she communicated the seriousness of having a relationship with God. As for my father, who is no longer living, I believe he would be proud of his children. Not because of any accomplishments we've made but because we are followers of God.

Surely, that was the point Joshua was making in Joshua 4:6 when at the direction of God, he asked the tribal leaders to take a stone and set up a memorial to remind future generations of the miraculous wonder of God as he cut off the waters of the Jordan to let the children of Israel pass over.

To those of us who have children, they ought to see us pray individually and as a family. Furthermore, don't let them take for granted the food that is placed before them especially when there are those who have none. Moreover, there ought to be an expectation that scripture is the final authority in their life. Planting God in the hearts of our children when they are young will yield great fruit in the future. This allows us to make the correlation between what we leave to our children and what God has left to us.

Remember God has an inheritance for you

Typically we define inheritance as receiving material possessions and or wealth at the time of a parent's death. Moreover, it can be defined as the transmission of genetic characters from parent to offspring.

After the conquest of many nations, the Lord informs Joshua (see Joshua chapter 13-21) that he is old and advanced in years, and there is still much land to possess. He reports to Joshua the regions that still need to be conquered but after that is completed; He wants Joshua to start the process of land distribution to the nine tribes of Israel and the half tribe of Manasseh.

While the biblical text shows God fulfilling his promise to Israel, I believe he desires to give much more than that. God wants his characteristics to be imbedded in our heart; that far outweighs what we can receive physically or monetarily.

I often hear people who proclaim the gospel speak solely of gaining material wealth when praying to God. They suggest that God doesn't want anyone to be broke. Consequently, we have a generation of Christians seeking the hand of God and not his face. In other words, we treat God as our genie in the bottle. If he refuses to grant us our wishes, then we say God doesn't answer prayer. What a worldly distortion of God.

As I stated above, God wants to share his character with us. We should desire to be like God and see people as

God sees them. But we can't do that on our own. So he gives us the Holy Spirit to aid us in developing our character to be conformed into his image. Furthermore, the Holy Spirit is the guarantee that we will receive our inheritance (see Ephesians 1:13-14). What a joy to know what is awaiting us in heaven. There is nothing on earth that compares to what we will see when we get there.

Caleb is a great example of being obedient, faithful and patient with regard to trusting God to fulfill his promise. He was forty when they spied out the land of Canaan (see Numbers 13) and he was one of two people out of the twelve that were sent who came back with a favorable report. Because he believed they could conquer Canaan, Caleb said to Joshua at the age of 85. God promised me this land forty-five years ago. Give it to me.

Isn't it amazing how we lack the ability to wait for long periods of time? Children of God, all throughout scripture God never forgets a promise. Whatever he's promised you. He will do it. Just believe his word it will come to pass.

If you're like me, then you've doubted God on many occasions. Take this opportunity to repent and start again.

Renew your commitment to following God

In Joshua's farewell address to all of Israel (see Joshua 23:2, 14), he tells them "I am now old and well advanced in years. And you have seen all that the Lord your God has done to all these nations for your sake, for it is the Lord your God who has fought for you…that not one word has failed of all the good things that the Lord your God promised concerning you. All have come to pass for you; not one of them has failed." He goes on to say that a transgression of the covenant will result in God's anger towards you and you will perish quickly.

Finally, he gathers the elders, officers, heads, and judges in Shechem to give them a history lesson by recounting all God had done for them from the time of establishing the covenant with Abraham to their current position. In addition, Joshua encourages them not serve the gods their father's served on the other side and in Egypt. He says, "Serve the Lord." But he challenges them to examine their heart by saying if you think it's evil to serve the Lord then you must make a choice. But the choice I make for myself and my family is that we will serve the Lord. Israel responds in verses 16-19 "Far be it from us that we should forsake the Lord to serve other gods, for it is the Lord our God who brought us and our fathers up from the land of Egypt, out of the house of slavery, and who did those great signs in our sight and preserved us in all the way that we went, and among all the peoples through whom we passed. And the Lord drove out before us all the peoples, the Amorites who lived in the land. Therefore, we also will serve the Lord, for he is our God."

Joshua like many of us is familiar with Israel's inconsistent affirmations during their journey to the promise land. He was there as the multitude made the exodus of out Egypt. He recalled the complaining when there was no bread or water. He heard the constant murmurings about Moses leading them to this desert place and their desire to return to Egypt because they were better off there. He was there when the people told Aaron to erect gods that they should go before and worship. He also witnessed God's judgment and mercy towards Israel. But he says again, in verse 20 "If you forsake the Lord and serve foreign gods, then he will turn and do you harm and consume you, after having done you good"

The almighty God wants you to remember all the things he's done for you. All the prayers he answered that you did not pray. He wants you to know that he heard your cries in the midnight when no one else could hear you. He understands the trouble you're in. But he requires obedience from you (see Isaiah 59:1-2).

As you aspire to renew your commitment to God, ask him not to allow the pressures of life to squeeze the very life out of you. And not let you be preoccupied with trying to achieve the fragmented American dream. Petition him to remove any relationships that don't have his approval. Request him to fan it into a raging flame your desire to passionately pursue him while allowing it to engulf others around you. And finally, profess to yourself and to others that the Lord sits on the throne of your heart. After you've done this, then you must realize that you are a witness against yourself.

Realize that your words will testify against you

In a court of law it's rare that an attorney will allow their client to testify in defense of themselves unless their testimony will change the outcome of the case. It is often reported that when clients take the stand to tell their account they dig a deeper hole for themselves and bring about a guilty verdict.

In Joshua's final remarks to the children of Israel in Joshua 24:22 he says, "You are witnesses against yourselves that you have chosen the Lord, to serve him. And they said we are witnesses." Therefore he say put away the foreign gods and draw near to the Lord, the God of Israel. Joshua then instructs them to take a large stone and set it under terebinth tree located by the sanctuary of the Lord as another witness against them. Assuming you were observing this closing argument as a juror, your verdict would be guilty. The children of Israel along with you and I have no excuse if we fall back into serving other gods. Let me conclude this chapter by saying what I said in the beginning, *serve the Lord!*

*i*Think Activation

After reading this chapter it's time to evaluate your servant hood relationship with the Lord. Looking at each of the six principles discussed in the chapter, how can you strengthen those areas. Write it in the space below and commit to work on it with God.

Re-acquaint us with the God of the Bible

_____

_____

_____

_____

Recognize the severity of sin

_____

_____

_____

_____

Recite God's goodness to your children

_____

_____

_____

_____

Remember God has an inheritance for you

_____

_____

_____

_____

Renew your commitment to following God

_____

_____

_____

_____

Realize the Bible will be a witness against you

_____

_____

_____

_____

Prayer: Lord, I'm amazed by your patience with fickle people like us who go back and forth with our word. One moment we are proclaiming your goodness and the next we're complaining about your provision. Lord please forgive us and help us to remain faithful to you just as you are faithful to us. Let me never forget to *"Serve the Lord,"* Amen.

6

*i*TH**NK

DON'T BE DISTRACTED

"For a small reward, a man will hurry away on a long journey; while for eternal life, many will hardly take a single step."

Thomas a' Kempis (1380-1471)

Why do the insignificant things consume the majority of our time while the consequential issues get the least amount? In some way, I believe that's the point Thomas a' Kempis is making in the above statement.

On October 13th, twenty-four days before the 2012 Presidential election. As a norm, at the start of the campaign both candidates relentlessly try to persuade the American voters that they are the best man for the job. We see their advertisements and public addresses that portray them in a positive light. We watch the live debates with the desire to be present while also participating in the political jousting between parties. Nonetheless, I believe these are only distractions motivated to take you away from the main point. It's been stated over the years by numerous individuals, we ought to keep the main thing, the main thing. But aren't we all guilty of this strategy, especially in our marriages, workplace environments, and churches?

Let me say, we are not alone. The Biblical account of Mary and Martha records the sisters having an opportunity that many of us long for and that is, to have Jesus Christ come to our home. The story tells us that when Jesus came into their home Mary sat at his feet and listened to his teaching while Martha was focused on serving and making sure everything was ready. Normally that is the correct response when inviting someone into your home in order that you're not viewed as inhospitable. But Jesus sees this encounter very differently. So in effort to fulfill the above command *"Don't be distracted,"* Here are three principles that will help guide us to fight off distractions when they come. The first thing you must do is; welcome God into your home, secondly, worship God as his disciple, and finally, acknowledge that worry minimizes the main point.

Welcome God into your house

Inviting someone into your home was not unusual for 1st century believers. As a matter of fact, it was the duty of the host to provide something to refresh their guest after a journey. Unlike in our present day society, some people don't open their homes to anyone for one reason or another. They quarantine themselves behind gated communities and participate in social solitude.

Welcoming persons into your home affords you an opportunity to engage in fellowship. Usually, when food is involved it helps facilitate the communication process. But asking Jesus to come into your home is no small matter. And some of you may be saying my home is full of dysfunction, arguments, negligence, and disappointments; why would God want to come into an environment such as mine? Because it's the perfect place for God to accomplish his will.

As he comes to Martha's house she does what anyone of us would do, she focuses on making a good impression. Countless individuals in our society don't want to be viewed in the wrong way. We mask who we are for the sake of embarrassment. But Jesus wants to see the real you, the naked you, the person you hide from others. He can help you if you're honest with him and with yourself.

Once more, what would Jesus see if he came to your home? Would you just keep him confined to the living room or would you allow him to have all access? But greater than our home is our heart and God wants all access to that area as well. He wants to see the secrets places, the sins, hurts, pains, and frustrations. But what he doesn't want to see is his children focusing on the trivial things of the world. Ironically, in Luke 10:39 we see two different approaches taken by these sisters. Mary is worshiping while Martha is working. God wants us to be aware that being his presence requires our un-divided attention.

How often are we too busy with the work of God that we miss ministry to God. As leaders, professionals and believers in general, our first ministries have to be to God and not for God. Ministry to God is that personal worship where we develop an intimate relationship with the Father. It's that uninterrupted time you give to God where he transforms your heart and your thinking. You cannot have true relationship without intimacy. How often have you bypassed time with God for church work? How many times did you walk past ministry on the way to do ministry.

It's time for a transformation in thinking. As God to help you slow down and maximize the moments of intimacy you have with the Lord. Be sensitive to those tugs on your heart to spend those extra moments basking in his presence.

Life is messy. You are going to have mess in your life that requires clean up. Refuse to allow yourself to run from God. Be aware of when you're only letting him into the living room of your life, you know those public places where we perpetuate that everything is okay. Undiscovered issues go unhealed. Let God discover your wounds, your hurt, your past and your pain. In his presence is the safest place to let your guard down and pour your heart out.

Worship God as his disciple

Jesus was a profound teacher; who captivated his listeners and aggravated his opponents. His popularity grew as the people witnessed the many miracles. Wherever he went multitudes followed and listened for hours. And it was no different with this single woman in attendance, this was the ultimate singles conference.

The Bible says, when Jesus entered Martha's home, Mary sat at his feet and listened to his teaching. Sitting at someone's feet meant that you were taking the posture of humility and learning. To receive one on one teaching from Jesus as a woman was uncommon in that day. But how awesome it was for Mary to relinquish all her worries and responsibilities and to solely focus on Jesus and what he said. There is a poem by an unknown author that expresses the essence of this story.

Martha in the kitchen, serving with her hands,
Occupied for Jesus with her pots and pans.
Loving Him, yet fevered, burdened to the brim,
Careful, troubled Martha, occupied for Him.

Mary on the footstool, eyes upon her Lord,
Occupied with Jesus, drinking in His word.

This one thing was needful, all else strangely dim;
Loving, resting Mary, occupied with Him.

So may we, like Mary, choose the better part:
Resting in His presence, hands and feet and heart;
Drinking in His wisdom, strengthened by His grace;
Waiting for the summons, eyes upon His face.

When it comes, we're ready, spirit, will, and nerve;
Mary's heart to worship, Martha's hand to serve;
This the rightful order, as our lamps we trim:
Occupied WITH Jesus, then occupied FOR Him!"

Oh saints of God, let us draw near to the Savior with our hearts and our mouths. Not only must we be disciples, but we must go make disciples. Have you spent enough time in the presence of the Lord to teach others what they must do? Are you able to give a credible defense to those who oppose the validity of Jesus Christ? If you lack the ability to give a proper defense of the gospel take Paul's advice to Timothy. He says in 2 Timothy 2:15 "Do your best to present yourself to God as one approved, a worker who has no need to be ashamed, rightly handling the word of truth." Finally, we need to keep in mind the main point and let nothing deter us.

Acknowledge that worry minimizes the main point

Upon Jesus' arrival to Martha's home, she begins the dutiful task of making Jesus' stay a pleasant one. As one could imagine, there is much to be done but Martha insists on Mary helping her. Maybe they discussed the responsibilities each would have once Jesus entered the home. But as soon as Mary sees Jesus she's so enamored by his presence that she forgoes the previous plans made. Therefore, Martha complains to Jesus about Mary's lack of participation. She says, "Lord, do you not care that my sister has left me to serve alone? Tell her then to help me." Jesus says her, "Martha, Martha, you are anxious and troubled about many things, but one thing is necessary, Mary has chosen the good portion, which will not be taken away from her." In other words, Jesus is not going to tell Mary to leave his presence in order to serve. Are you worried, preoccupied, or troubled about a situation in your life? Remember you have Jesus right there in your presence ask him to help you.

One of the most debilitating diseases that affect the believer is the disease of worry. Worry and anxiety go hand in hand. Oftentimes, we can be so anxious about an issue that it makes us believe that we are having a heart attack. Moreover, worry and anxiety stem from a lack of trust. As Jesus stated to Martha, "You are anxious and troubled about many things."

What is causing you to worry today? Is it your finances, marital status, children, etc.? The cause is irrelevant. Jesus wants you and me to take the posture of Mary, which is to sit and listen to his instruction.

The Apostle Paul also addressed the issue of anxiety to the church at Philippi. He says in Philippians 4:6 "do not be anxious about anything, but in everything by prayer and supplication with thanksgiving let your requests be made known to God. And the peace of God, which surpasses all understanding, will guard your hearts and your minds in Christ Jesus." I heard a preacher say one time as he was expounding on this verse; that the devil always wants us to be feeling what we are thinking and to be thinking about what we are feeling; therefore keeping us in a vicious cycle but the remedy is to pray and offer supplication with thanksgiving to God. And he will guard our minds, which are the source of our thoughts, and our heart, which is the seat of our emotions this will break that cycle. Give every worry to God and he will take care of you and your problem.

Worrying, the Gospel writer Matthew says, it can't add a single hour to your life span; however, our focus should be to seek first the Kingdom of God and he righteousness and God will take care of the rest. To trust is the ability to give it to God and know he will come through. That's the point Jesus wanted Martha to see. His presence brought with it fullness of joy forever more. Keep the main point the main point, which is Jesus.

Finally, Charles Spurgeon the prince of preachers said in his Morning and Evening devotion, "he who has been with us in six troubles will not forsake us in the seventh." Those are words that we should carry with us every day. Don't let anything distract us from God.

*i*Think Activation

Have you been busy doing the work of ministry for God to where you are missing the precious moments of ministry to God? Reflect on where you are in your relationship with God and then use the space below to commit to more uninterrupted personal time with God.

_____
_____
_____
_____
_____
_____
_____
_____
_____
_____
_____
_____

Prayer: Lord, life presents many of us with challenges, some we think we can handle and others that are overwhelming. Help me to recognize that these are only distractions that come to get my attention diverted from the main point, which is worshiping you. I submit myself to your will your way and acknowledge that nothing else matters, Amen.

7

*i*THINK

LOOK UP!

"Post Tenebrous Lux"---"After Darkness...Light"
John Calvin the Great Reformer

Darkness is often communicated and illustrated in a myriad of ways. There are those who've expressed in great times of despair of being in a dark place. I personally can attest to that as well. When you're in that place, it seems as if no one else can identify with you. You feel all alone as if abandoned in the ocean with no civilization or land in sight. Some can affirm darkness to be a garment so heavy that without help they can't remove it.

In the above quote by John Calvin, he states without stating, the liberty light brings to change a situation. This great reformer was born in 1509 in Geneva Switzerland; during a time when there was no water inside homes, no antibiotics to cure illnesses, corporal punishment was being burned alive at the stake for your beliefs and a man could have one mistress in addition to his wife. This doesn't sound much different from what we are experiencing in modern day society. With all the moral corruptness then and now, there's still hope and consolation for the world. This hope will not be achieved by human efforts alone, but will take a divine intervention.

The Bible proclaims that God is light and in him there is no darkness at all. So the question becomes, what is darkness? Is it simply the absence of Light? Or, in addition to what has been described above, can it be conveyed as being without understanding? Has someone ever told you that you were intentionally kept in the dark on a particular issue? God doesn't want any of his children to be left in the dark. He wants them to be illumined by his Word however, to escape this darkness of understanding one must *"Look Up."*

Looking up is not just a movement of the head to see the stars in the sky, but a voluntary act, which says, there is help beyond the clouds. Maybe you don't consider yourself to be religious but sometimes life hands you difficult challenges that move you to say, "If there is a God, can you help me?"

I'm currently dealing with a difficult challenge in my life and over the past couple of weeks I've felt as if God had left me. I struggled with the question of why. Why God are you allowing me to continue to experience disappointment in such a dramatic way? Like many believers who walk with God, I have battled depression, frustration, and even thoughts of ending it all. But the other night, I was speaking to a newly found friend who helped shine some light on my situation. She stated, often times, believers do not want to go through any hardship. They expect the journey of life to be without difficulties. She also stated, life's intense struggles are like the birth pains a woman experiences as she is about to bring life into the world. The pain starts out infrequent then it progresses with intensity and frequency. As the woman continues to push through the threshold she then receives a gift that causes her to forget about the tears and anguish she just experienced.

As we continue to live, we must realize that suffering is a part of life. No matter how intense the struggle God is always there with us. Unfortunately, the Christian community has been duped into believing the reason for their trials is due to a lack of faith but that's not true it's just the opposite. Trials come to increase our faith and help us see God's power in a different way. As we are maneuvering through this maze of life, God lets us know that this is all a part of a greater plan for our lives. Like you, sometimes I can stand tall in that truth, but then there are times when it's not as easy. There are moments where I want to scream, "I don't want this greater plan God has for me. I need a break from all of this!" It is in those moments, that the Holy Spirit reminds me that God my father will never leave me nor will he forsake me and it encourages me.

God has not forgotten you. He has not walked away from you in times of trouble. He stands complete and confident in his word to encourage you to keep moving. The wonderful thing about God is that He never points more on you than you can bear. If you got it, you can handle it.

The Psalm 121:1-8 answers the question, Where does my help come from when I'm in trouble? This Psalm gives us five prescriptive measures to aid us in obtaining victory over our circumstances.

- ♈ The creator of the universe helps me
- ♈ The creator of the universe keeps me planted
- ♈ The creator of the universe does not sleep
- ♈ The creator of the universe keeps me from all evil
- ♈ The creator of the universe keeps my life eternal

The Creator of the universe helps me

The Psalmist says I look up to the hills, from where does my help come from? It's not as though he doesn't know because he answers the question in verse 2, "my help comes from the Lord." He doesn't leave the Lord undefined; he identifies the Lord as the creator of the heavens and the earth. You and I must know the only God that can help us is the one who created all things. Also, contrary to the claims of other religions we do not serve the same God. Allah, Buddha, or any other names that cultic religions try to impose on us are not the true God. The God of the Bible as identified in this Psalm and in multiple places throughout scripture is the only one that can and will deliver you from all your problems. Again, be confident that no matter how it looks, God will help you despite the severity and or longevity of the problem. He not only will help me but he will also keep my feet from being moved.

The Creator of the universe keeps me planted

There are some translations that read Psalm 121:3 as "He will not let your foot be moved" and others that read, "May he not let your foot be moved" whichever way you read it the bottom line is that God is in control whether he allows it or not.

Asaph reminds us in Psalm 73:2 of the realization that God knows what's going on in your life. He writes, "But as for me, my feet had almost stumbled, my steps had nearly slipped..." The reason for this near slip lies within what he perceived the unrighteous getting away with. He says they experience no physical maladies until it's time to die; they curse heaven and wear pride as a necklace. How many of us wonder, why do the righteous get what the wicked deserve and the wicked get what the righteous deserve? Well Asaph finds the answer when he enters the sanctuary of God. He discovers and writes in Psalm 73:18, that God has them on a slippery slope. And he'll make them fall to ruin and they'll be destroyed in a moment. So child of God remember whatever is out of order, whatever is not fair, and whatever seems chaotic, God knows all about it.

You may have a mindset to give up right now or you may be saying, what's the use all I've seen is trouble. My encouragement to you is not to give up on God because Jude 1: 24 states "Now to him who is able to keep you from stumbling and to present you blameless before the presence of his glory with great joy, to the only God, our Savior, through Jesus Christ our Lord, be glory, majesty, dominion, and authority, before all time and now and forever. Amen." Our third prescriptive measure informs us that you can call on God any time of day or night.

The Creator of the universe doesn't sleep

The Psalmist says that our Lord the Creator of the universe never sleeps nor does he slumber. What a great assurance we have as believers. We can approach God morning, noon, or night and God is there to hear our problems, petitions, and worries. But at times you wonder just as I do, does he really hear me? Does he care about what I'm going through? My answer to you is yes he cares. If he is concerned about the flower in the field as Matthew's gospel says then surely he's concerned about you and me.

Our faith must be in the fact that though he does not answer us when we think he should he hears the cry of his children. As a parent I don't always answer my children's every request. For instance, I could be watching T.V. when my two-year-old daughter comes to me and ask for some cookies, I hear her request but if I don't respond she says daddy continuously until I say yes sweetie, then she says, "Can I have some cookies."

How can I deny her request? Now if I can do that, how much more will our Heavenly Father answer his children? Rest assured beloved, he hears everything. It doesn't matter the volume of the request, God hears and will answer but we must be patient for his response. Our fourth prescriptive measure promises us that he will keep us from all evil.

The Creator of the universe keeps us from all evil

What does the Psalmist mean when he says he will keep us from all evil; he will keep your life? This speaks of God's preservation of his people. We cannot keep ourselves. The ability to keep us belongs to God and God alone. It's his power that keeps us from sinning. It's not how much we pray, fast, or attend church.

Many of us are familiar with the story when Abraham told his wife Sarah to say she was his sister at the time they were in Gerar in Genesis 20:1-18. Consequently, King Abimelech took Sarah to be one of his slaves. Genesis 20:3 goes on to say, "But God came to Abimelech in a dream by night and said to him, Behold, you are a dead man because the woman whom you have taken, for she is a man's wife. Now Abimelech had not approached her. So he said, Lord, will you kill an innocent people? Did he not himself say to me, she is my sister? And she herself said, He is my brother. In the integrity of my heart and the innocence of my hands I have done this. Then God said to him in the dream, Yes, I know that you have done this in the integrity of your heart, and it was I who kept you from sinning against me. Therefore I did not let you touch her."

Beloved God has the power to prohibit anyone from sinning or sinning against his people.

Has there been a time in your life that you planned out a particular sin, you made the call, everything was in motion but it never came to pass? It was God who keep you from sinning and kept your life while ensuring you would not sin against him. How great is the God of the universe? Finally, the last prescription of victory reassures us that the Lord will keep us forever and forevermore.

The Creator of the universe will keep my life eternally

Although this is the last verse of this Psalm it's also the climax. How great and precious is this promise of God's keeping power? The Psalmist says, "The Lord will keep & protect your going out and your coming in not just forever but forevermore." You can hang your hat on God's promises. Moses reassures us in Numbers 23:19 "God is not a man that he should lie, or a son of man, that he should change his mind. Has he said, and will he not do it? Or has he spoken, and will he not fulfill it? Oh children of the most the high, hide these words in your heart so when doubt arises you can bring it to the forefront, speak it to yourself, and believe that your faith will increase and endure. Our problems don't move God. He knows what's going on he's not out of the loop on anything that transpires in our lives, all he wants us to do is *"Look Up."*

*i*Think Activation

Examine where you are in your life right now. Where do you need to *"Look Up"* in your life. Write about where you are and commit to give God "keeping" power of the things that have kept you bound.

_____

_____

_____

_____

_____

_____

_____

_____

_____

_____

_____

Prayer: Lord, let us remember the words of the wisest man that ever lived King Solomon; In Ecclesiastes 7:14 he says "In the day of prosperity be joyful, and in the day of adversity consider: God has made the one as well as the other, so that man may not find out anything that will be after him." My father, I accept the good and the bad in my life but I cast it at your feet knowing you will not allow me to be overwhelmed by life's blessings or obstacles. Thank you for your grace, Amen.

8

*i*THINK

ONLY BELIEVE

*It must grieve the heart of God that he delivers us
through so many things and when we come to the next
thing; we act as if he has never delivered us!*

*Dr. Gardner C. Taylor, Pastor Emeritus
Concorde Baptist Church, Brooklyn, New York*

The mounting challenges that confront us daily often cause us to doubt the validity of a caring God. But it's not until we get through the difficult challenge that we reflect and realize God has been with us every step of the way. How can God be ever-present but make you feel as if he's absent? How can he walk with us and see danger and sometimes not warn us but pick us up and carry us through while we're feeling we've been in it all by ourselves? I call that amazing.

It does not matter the length of time you've been walking with God, but what matters is are you learning what he's been trying to teach you? The repetitiveness of a test might suggest our disobedience to his will, while the deluge of trouble you're experiencing can also be attributed to God wanting to receive glory from your life.

An astonishing story arises out of the text in the gospel of Mark chapter 5. This story conveys the desperate longing of a father who needs Jesus to do something that has not been done since the Old Testament. It's been 400 years since God spoke or did anything miraculous. Now we see a ruler of the synagogue amongst the crowd anxiously anticipating the arrival of Jesus from the other side to perform miracles they only read and heard about.

Has there been a time in your life that you needed Jesus so badly you were willing to bombard heaven with your continued request? It didn't matter your status or degrees you became like everyone else, a beggar to the one who could solve the problem. Jairus' status meant nothing at that moment yet he gives us some practical ways to assist in fulfilling the command to "Only believe." I'll call them the 6 W's, worship, want, wait, waste, weeping, and wonder.

There must be WORSHIP

Jairus was the ruler of the Jewish synagogue; which means he presided over the local synagogue while also supervising the worship. This man falls at Jesus' feet. He moves from supervising worship to engaging in worship. Although, in today's society people in local congregations view the pastor as one, who does not go through problems, doesn't need any counseling, family is always doing well, and who does not experience the internal battles with sin. But that's not true. We constantly hear of preachers falling prey to the attacks of the enemy or even experiencing self inflicted wounds; which is an indication of an acute need of Jesus' intervention. Worship should be a vital part of the believers' life. Not one day should pass without you or me taken part in meaningful worship and acknowledging the awe of this great God.

Since Jairus is a ruler of the synagogue, he's intimately aware of the Old Testament prophecies that proclaim the Messiah comes to heal, deliver, and open blinded eyes. So now we find him worshiping and then offering up his petition to the Lord Jesus Christ.

There must be a WANT

It is safe to say that everyone who comes to Jesus wants something from him. If we didn't, we simply wouldn't come. Would you go to someone who couldn't do anything for you? Of course not, there must be a pressing need in your life in order for you to seek help from another person. The Bible is packed full of persons coming to Jesus because they had a want or a need; consequently, the motive of an individual must be examined.

Unfortunately, we see it happening every Sunday in churches across America, persons coming to Jesus to escape their troubles because they heard the preacher say "If you come to Jesus he'll fix all your problems." therefore producing false converts. But when their problems get increasingly worse they leave the church and say, "I knew there was nothing to this Jesus stuff."

As we witness to those around us, it's important to provide them with sound Biblical truth and understanding, in the meanwhile, producing a true convert. Jairus trusted in the Old Testament and believed if God did it for the ancient Jews surely he can do it for me. And that should be our attitude; if he did it for those in scripture then he'll do it for me. After hearing his request he follows the ruler to his house but on the way Jesus encounters a woman who takes what she needs from him which causes him to pause before proceeding with Jairus'.

You must WAIT

We live in a world full of impatient people who want everything right now. The ability to wait is not a natural behavior for most people. Even for the Christian, waiting can be one of the most aggravating times our life. Although we sing songs that proclaim to the world our ability to wait on God, we exhibit behavior that opposes our proclamation. The reason for this response is that we've placed God on a time schedule. If he doesn't answer within our set time, then we start to complain, get frustrated, and doubt his ability altogether. On the other hand, we must ask ourselves, how can the clay say to the potter why haven't you answered? Who are we to question God's timetable? Could you imagine being in Jairus' shoes at this moment?

Jesus agrees to go with him and heal his daughter; however the crowd wanted to follow as well. As they proceed, a woman makes her way through all the people to touch just a part of his clothing in hopes of her receiving what she needs. Then Jesus stops. I can only imagine the sense of urgency that was looming in the heart of Jairus. Come on Jesus we must get to my daughter before something worse happens! Keep in mind; Jesus will take the time to deal with every request asked in faith. Don't worry about the delay it doesn't mean God has denied you. Now while Jesus deals with the woman who touches him, Jairus receives word not to bother the Master any longer, your daughter is dead! See Mark 5:35. The fourth W calls for us not to waste anymore of God's time.

Don't WASTE God's time

What a devastating blow Jairus receives from those who had been watching the demise of his daughter. Could you imagine how his heart must have sank within him. If is had been me in this passage, my reaction would have been, Jesus, why did you stop? I'm sure many of us can identify with that statement. We believe God for a miracle and suddenly it turns for the worst. And we say in our hearts "No need to waste God's time any longer it's over" But despite the gravity of the situation the consolation comes in verse 36 "But overhearing what they said, Jesus said to the ruler of the synagogue, do not fear… only believe."

Don't let your heart sink to believe that at someone else's word, your situation cannot turn around. God is just as interested in your life as he is in others. You are not wasting God's time; He always has enough time for you. Keep the faith and stand on his word it will come out in your favor. Don't listen to the doubters or even those who come with practical wisdom. Listen to the one who is in control of the universe and know that nothing takes him by surprise. He knew people were coming to give him bad news yet sometimes God won't step into your situation until he knows that nothing humanly possible can be done. What an assurance we have in God. Even when things appear to be dead, we must know that we serve a God who has resurrection power. However, it doesn't mean you won't shed any tears along the journey.

There will be WEEPING

So as Jesus proceeds to the ruler's house with only Peter, James, and John, he notices a lot of commotion taking place. As he enters and sees those weeping and wailing, he asks what some might call a dumb question; what's going on here and why are you all crying? Can you imagine the look of shock on their faces when they heard this? By the way, it was not unusual for outside or professional mourners to be present at a time like this, at the same time, some of those mourners might have stopped crying and said "Is this guy serious?" then resumed their crying.

Nevertheless, what you and I must come to realize about Jesus is his questions are much deeper than they appear and his answers more profound than we think. As Jesus follows his question with the response of "she is not dead but sleeping" they burst into laughter then Jesus puts them all out with the exception of the parents and those he brought with him.

The principle to be learned here is when you need something from God it is imperative to have those around you who believe and agree in faith with you. If they do not or cannot believe, then it is best not to have them around while you believe God for a particular miracle. After you've worshiped, wanted, waited, wasted and wept then God does a wonder.

There will be a WONDER

Jesus the miracle worker brings those who believed with him to the place where the child was and took her by the hand simply saying, "Talitha cumi," which means, "little girl, I say to you arise." Allow God to speak to whatever is dead in your life whether it is your finances, marriage, children or even your church. When God speaks, everything has to listen and respond. Nothing can stop Jesus. He has all authority in heaven and in earth (see Matthew 28:18).

I know your situation may look and feel dead but God's word to you is "Do not fear, only believe." Receive that word into your heart. And you will experience the wonder of God.

*i*Think Activation

It's time to believe God for a miracle. What needs to be resurrected from the dead? What feels impossible? Where do you need God to show up in your life? It's time to stop, drop and believe God to make your life a wonder and a miracle.

_____

_____

_____

_____

_____

_____

_____

_____

_____

_____

_____

Prayer: Dear Lord, the words "Do not fear, only believe" are words to live by, never let me doubt your authority and power in my life. May I always trust in you, In Jesus name, Amen.

9

*i*THINK

TAKE DAVID WITH YOU

"No man is a failure who has friends"
Frank Capra's "It's A Wonderful Life"

One of the most intriguing and inspiring stories of friendship I've read in the Bible is the story of Jonathan and David. These two warriors expressed their heartfelt devotion to one another despite opposition from family, servants and enemies. The word loyalty comes to mind to describe what they had but more importantly they had a reverence for the one true God of Israel.

How is it that we don't see this type of friendship in today's world? Could it be that we choose our friends based on the benefit we receive from them or they from us? Or is it because we only want people in our lives that always see us as right even if we're wrong? Those individuals are not considered to be friends but leaches or yes men. However, that wasn't the case with Jonathan and David. Here we have two men with similar qualities. They were men of valor, men of war, prudent in speech, and men of good presence, and the Lord was with them (1 Samuel 16:18).

On the other hand, what would make a prince whose next in line for the throne choose to befriend a man who seemingly has the pulse of the people over his father? And it is apparent that if a vote were cast they would reject both father and son while choosing this man. 1 Sam. 18:7 says "And the women sang to one another as they celebrated, Saul has struck down his thousands, and David his ten thousands."

I believe the answer can be found in the character qualities that Jonathan saw in David and that we must see in those whom we choose to be our friends. In the process of *"Taking David with you,"* here are the character qualities we need to see in others and ourselves if they are to travel with us on this journey of life:

- ♈ A Love relationship with God
- ♈ Live for God
- ♈ Be bold for God
- ♈ Give to God

A love relationship with God

When Saul was rejected as King of Israel, the Lord sent the Prophet Samuel to the house of Jesse to anoint the next king. He would not be chosen based on his looks or stature but by his heart. The process was simple, on whichever person the anointing oil was released; he would be God's chosen (see 1Samuel 16:1-13). God demonstrates to us in his choosing, that the exterior of a man doesn't matter but the true essence of a man is revealed by what's in his heart.

David had such a love relationship with God even at a young age and it was obvious that it was taught to him in the home. We need more parents teaching their children to love the Lord with all of their heart, soul, mind, and strength in this post-modern age. We try everything else before we try God.

As Samuel requests for David to pass under the horn of oil then we see God allowing the oil to be released on him which indicates to all present that God would be with him from that day forward. And so it is with the Holy Spirit that dwells in all believers, we have the assurance that he will never leave us nor will he abandon us. This love relationship is initiated and maintained by God therefore we must praise him for choosing us knowing we would fail on our end.

Jonathan and David's friendship was a typology of Christ and the church. The Bible makes it apparent that a friendship has a stronger tie than a family bond. Their relationship was not perverted, it was authentic and reflected the genuineness of one another. Are you able to be an authentic friend? Can you say you're in a love relationship with God? Hold your answer because the next character quality that a David in your life must possess is that of living for God.

Live for God

Have you encountered others who state how much they love the Lord but in their actions they are contradictory? I'm sure many of us would give a resounding "yes" to that question. But the next question is, why? After Samuel anointed David, The bible says in verse 13b of chapter 16 "And the Spirit of the Lord rushed upon David from that day forward." Could it be that our failures in living for God is due to the lack of acknowledging that the Lord is with us everywhere we go? Or does it show our lack of commitment towards him?

Life has a way of presenting us with some very difficult challenges from time to time and the reality is we don't always measure up. Your external self doesn't always reflect what's in your heart. However, thank God for his grace and mercy, which covers all our failures yet still, provides us with an opportunity to move in the right direction. Perfection is not what the Lord is looking for or else we all would be disqualified. He is simply looking for your availability.

As you live for God, don't discount who God brings around you as a friend simply because they don't measure up to your perceived reality. Just as God accepts you, just accept them for what's in their heart; God does. And that leads us to our third character quality that a David must possess boldness for God.

Be bold for God

As David gives his reason to King Saul for being qualified to fight Goliath, he reflects on a time when a bear and a lion tried to take sheep from the flock; he struck and killed them (see 1 Samuel 17: 32-37). This shepherd boy does not attribute his victory over these animals to his skill or wit he gives the credit to God. And furthermore he states that God will deliver this Philistine into his hands also.

What great confidence David has in God and how much more should we exude the same confidence because we serve the same God. The bible declares that, "the righteous are as bold as a lion (see Prov. 28:1)."

Just for a moment, put yourself in the story of David and Goliath. Can you imagine seeing this nine-foot giant scoffing at the army of Saul while they are in sheer terror and in hiding? Suddenly, you see this young kid whose only experience is fighting animals going down into the valley to fight a giant and his weapon of choice is a rock and a sling. Do you see what the God kind of boldness will do for you? Beloved, know that every encounter that comes your way God is with you and he will help you defeat the giants in your life. The last character quality that a David must possess is being a giver.

Give to God

Giving is a necessary part of life that requires an investment of our time, talent, and treasure. It also means that our word is at the root. In 1 Samuel 20:14-17 Jonathan asks David "never cutoff your steadfast love from my house forever even when the Lord cuts off everyone of your enemies from the face of the earth." Jonathan makes David swear again by his love for him that he will keep his promise. One thing God desires of us is to draw near to him with our heart instead of our mouths. We've been around people who give us lip service but never follow through. How does that make you feel? Just think of the times when you said to God I will do this or that but you never perform it. Despite your lack of follow through he's still there, listening and answering your prayers.

After the death of King Saul and his son Jonathan, David remembered his covenant with Jonathan. Jonathan had a son named Mephibosheth who was five when his father died. After God defeated David's enemies and years passed David asked is there anyone left of the house of Saul that I may show kindness to for Jonathan's sake? And Ziba who was a servant of Saul came to King David and said Jonathan has a son who is lame in his feet. David said to the servant bring him to me. So David said to Mephibosheth "Do not fear, for I will show you kindness for the sake of your father Jonathan, and I will restore to you all the land of Saul your father, and you shall eat at my table always...all that belonged to Saul and to all his house I give to you"

Just as David kept his word let's make it our business to keep our word to one another and to our heavenly father.

*i*Think Activation

Israel Houghton penned a song with lyrics that sign the heart of this chapter, "I am a friend of God." We must not only embrace our friendship with the Lord but see it as a schoolmaster for building healthy friendships rooted in loyalty, love, grace and commitment. Who has God placed in your life to be your Jonathan? Have you received them as God would want you to? Think on your friendships and write about how you can apply these principles to your present day friendships.

_____
_____
_____
_____
_____
_____
_____
_____
_____
_____
_____
_____

Prayer: Lord, help me to realize that the greatest friend I could have is you and you'll always keep your word. Thank you for being a great God, Amen.

10

i THINK

GOD DID IT

"In the day of prosperity be joyful, and in the day of adversity consider: God has made the one as well as the other…"

King Solomon

In life when people encounter trouble and significant trials, the devil is often the named culprit. It doesn't matter how trivial or complex the issue; it is believed without hesitance he orchestrated the disturbance in their life. However, the author of the trouble is not the devil. He simply carries out the order. So then, the question becomes who is the author of the turmoil you or I may be experiencing in our lives right now? The answer is God.

Within the human race many often express it when something good happens it's God and when it doesn't it is the devil. The way to transform this thinking is to have a proper understanding of the Sovereignty of God. The Sovereignty of God means that all things are under his rule and reign while nothing happens without his knowledge or authorization.

King Solomon the wisest man in the world offers us wisdom upon which we must reflect in the above quote from Ecclesiastes 7:14. He says, "The prosperity and adversity in a person's life comes from God." This belief is not solely confined within the book of Ecclesiastes, but is communicated throughout scripture.

The book of Genesis gives us a compelling account of the story of Joseph, whose troubles would have deterred a number of us from our continued pursuit of God's vision for our lives, but for him he realized it was God who authored everything to take place. And so it is with us, we must understand the troubles that come our way are simply tools from God to train us to become who he has destined us to be.

Joseph's story is not foreign to those of us who believe God has shown us something about our future and the people and circumstances along with ourselves who try to sabotage it. Say what you will about Joseph sharing his dream with his family, who wouldn't? How many times did you share something you believed was from God and didn't get the response you thought you should've? Or you shared something and sensed the jealousy coupled with alienation? God knew that would be the result. He simply uses those people and situations to teach us. Joseph's story gives us a valuable perspective to enhance our dependence on God.

His brothers stripped him of his coat of many colors, threw him into a pit, and sold him into slavery but God was using this as a means of preservation. Sometimes when God informs us of whom we are to become, he has to take us off the scene for a moment in order to develop us. If you're feeling as if you are in the background maybe it's because the Lord is developing you.

After his brothers sell him to the Ishmaelites for twenty shekels of silver which is equivalent to about 220-230 dollars. They sell him to Potiphar who was an officer of Pharaoh and captain of the guard. So he goes from the pit to Potiphar. Potiphar sees the Lord is with Joseph and realizes that he succeeds at whatever he does. Although it looks one way on the surface, I believe the reason he's in Potiphar's house is to learn how to resist temptation.

If God is in the process of elevating you then you must learn to resist temptation. It does not matter if you're being promoted on your job or in your church, temptation must be handled. The first verse of scripture I learned was 1 Corinthians 10:13, "No temptation has overtaken you that is not common to man, God is faithful, and he will not let you be tempted beyond your ability but with the temptation he will also provide the way of escape, that you may be able to endure it."

When the persistent wife of Potiphar confronted Joseph, he asked her a question in Genesis 39:9, "How then can I do this great wickedness and sin against God?" Beloved we must view sexual sin as Joseph did. We must do three things:

- ⚲ See it as a great wickedness
- ⚲ See it as sinning against God and
- ⚲ We must flee.

When you do the right thing, like Joseph, you may tell the truth and someone else release a false accusation against you. Joseph was wrongfully imprisoned at the words of Potiphar's wife. Although unfair, he goes from the pit to Potiphar's house then from Potiphar's house to prison.

Have you ever been falsely accused of something, but you have no way of proving your innocence? This is Joseph's case. It seems he can't get a break. Trouble back to back and I'm sure it felt over whelming. I've often expressed at times in my own situations "God you said I was going to receive double for my trouble but it seems like it's double trouble." In the face of adversity, we must understand through all of our trials, God is with us. No matter where we are in trouble, his favor is on us.

As the story continues, while Joseph is in prison unjustly, he encounters two individuals that need his help interpreting their dreams. He gives them the interpretation and asks the chief cupbearer to remember him when he is restored to his position. Isn't it ironic to be in place where you feel you need help but God sends people for you to help? And you ask God, when is help coming for me? Be encouraged and know that your help is on the way.

Joseph's help eventually came. It came two years later when Pharaoh had a dream and requested for someone to give the interpretation then the cupbearer remembered what Joseph did for him while they were in prison. Pharaoh called for Joseph. Now he moves from the prison to the palace. He interprets Pharaoh's dream and is placed second in command of all Egypt.

As we look at this story, it didn't happen overnight, it took 13 years for Joseph's vision to come to pass. All the while, through every phase of the journey the Lord was with him and God's favor was upon him. His testament to his brothers was don't be angry with yourselves God sent me before you to preserve life (see Genesis 45:5)

We often do not understand why God does what he does but I'm learning to say in my own life, God your will your way. We have to be BOLD enough to trust God where we can't trace him, RESILIANT enough to bounce back even when it seems like the plan isn't going the way we imagined and COURAGEOUS enough to go where others fear to experience the life most don't.

Within you is a clarion call to leadership. You may be leading a church, a family, a division in your company or simply your own life. No matter what you've been called to, there is a supernatural grace that comes when you let God's thoughts migrate to the mind of man. Put off the thoughts that keep you captive and inhibit your ability to lead with power and authority.

As a leader, you don't have all the answers, but you have access to the leader to leaders. Tap into that power and let it help you move forward in all that you were created to be. It is my prayer that this book will help you on your journey towards transformational thinking, which will result in Godly behaviors. Day by day, step by step...iThink your life will never be the same.

*i*Think Activation

By this point, there should have been some major moments of transformation that changed how you view God, yourself and the world around you. Reflect on what you've gained from this book and write down the ten thoughts that have changed through this journey, followed by your own personal prayer.

- *i*Think _____
- *i*Think _____
- *i*Think _____
- *i*Think _____
- *i*Think _____
- *i*Think _____
- *i*Think _____
- *i*Think _____
- *i*Think _____
- *i*Think _____

Prayer:

_____

_____

_____

_____

_____

_____

_____

_____

_____

_____

_____

_____

_____

_____

_____

_____

_____

_____

_____

_____

_____

_____

_____

_____

_____

ABOUT THE AUTHOR

Andre Dove is the Lead Pastor of Restoration Church in Spokane, WA; He holds a B.A. in Religion from Faith Evangelical College & Seminary in Tacoma, WA; He is currently pursuing a Masters in Theology with an emphasis in Urban Ministry from Grand Canyon University in Phoenix, AZ. He has four beautiful children.